AF256140

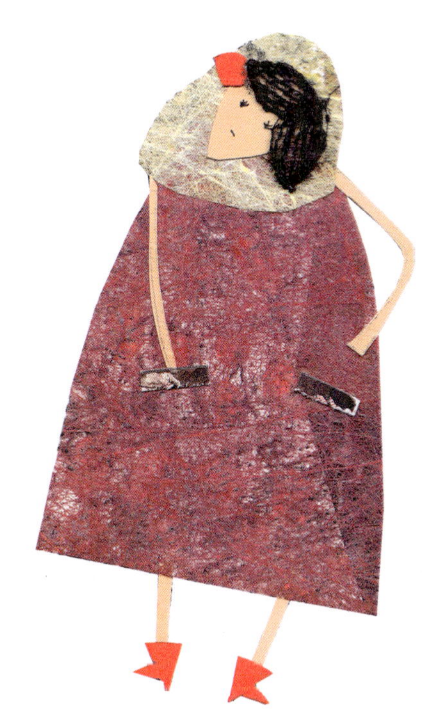

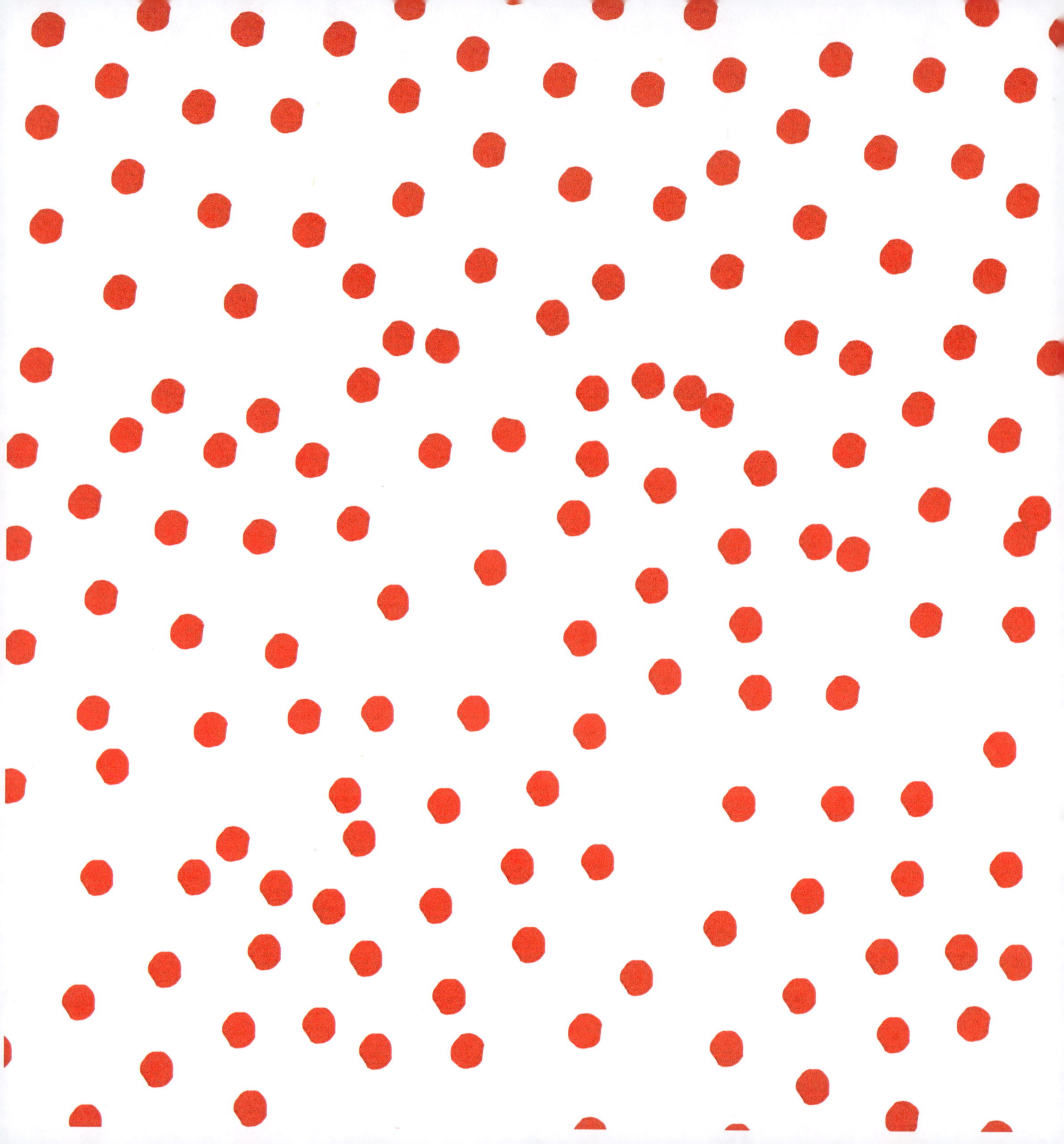

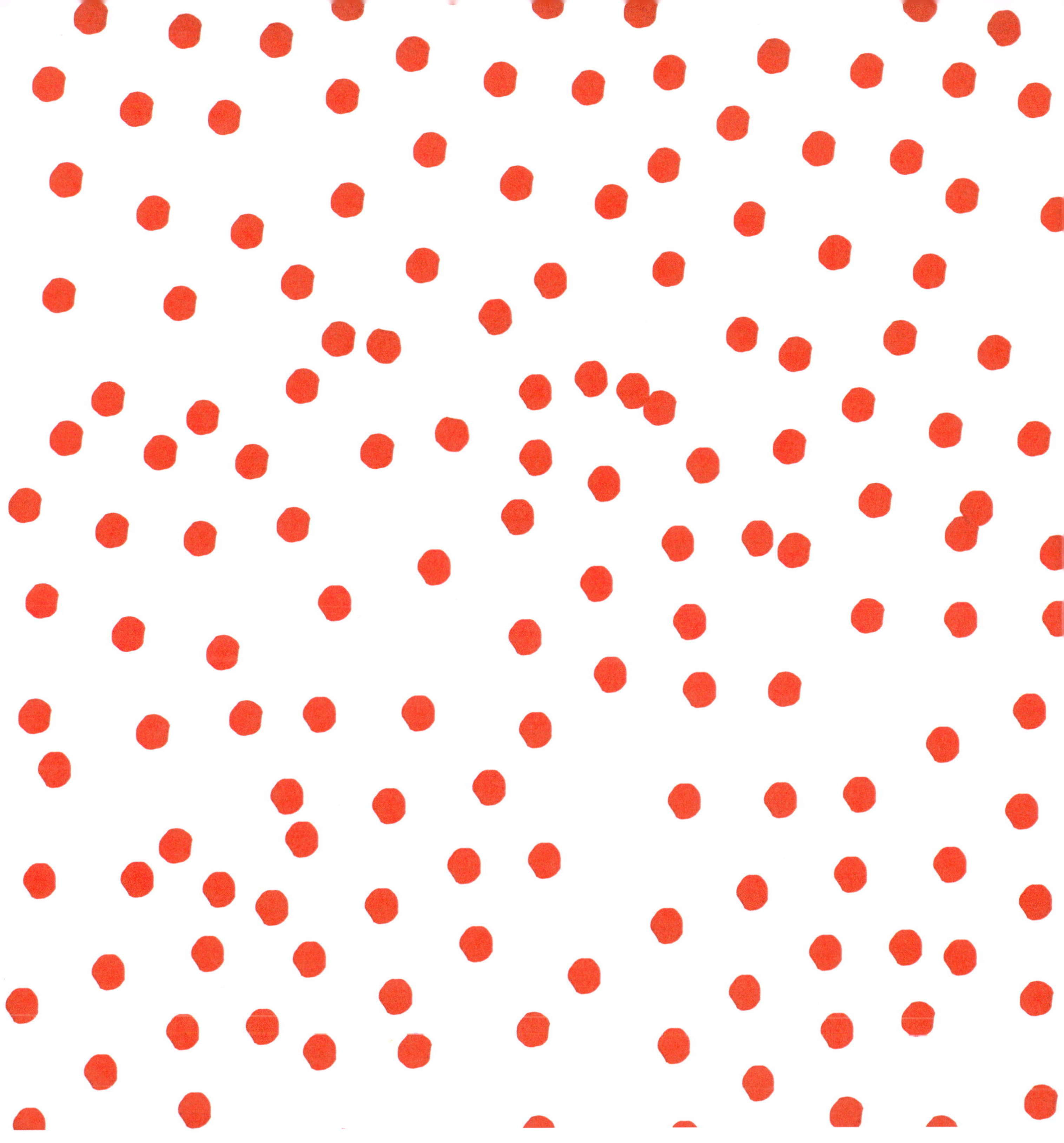

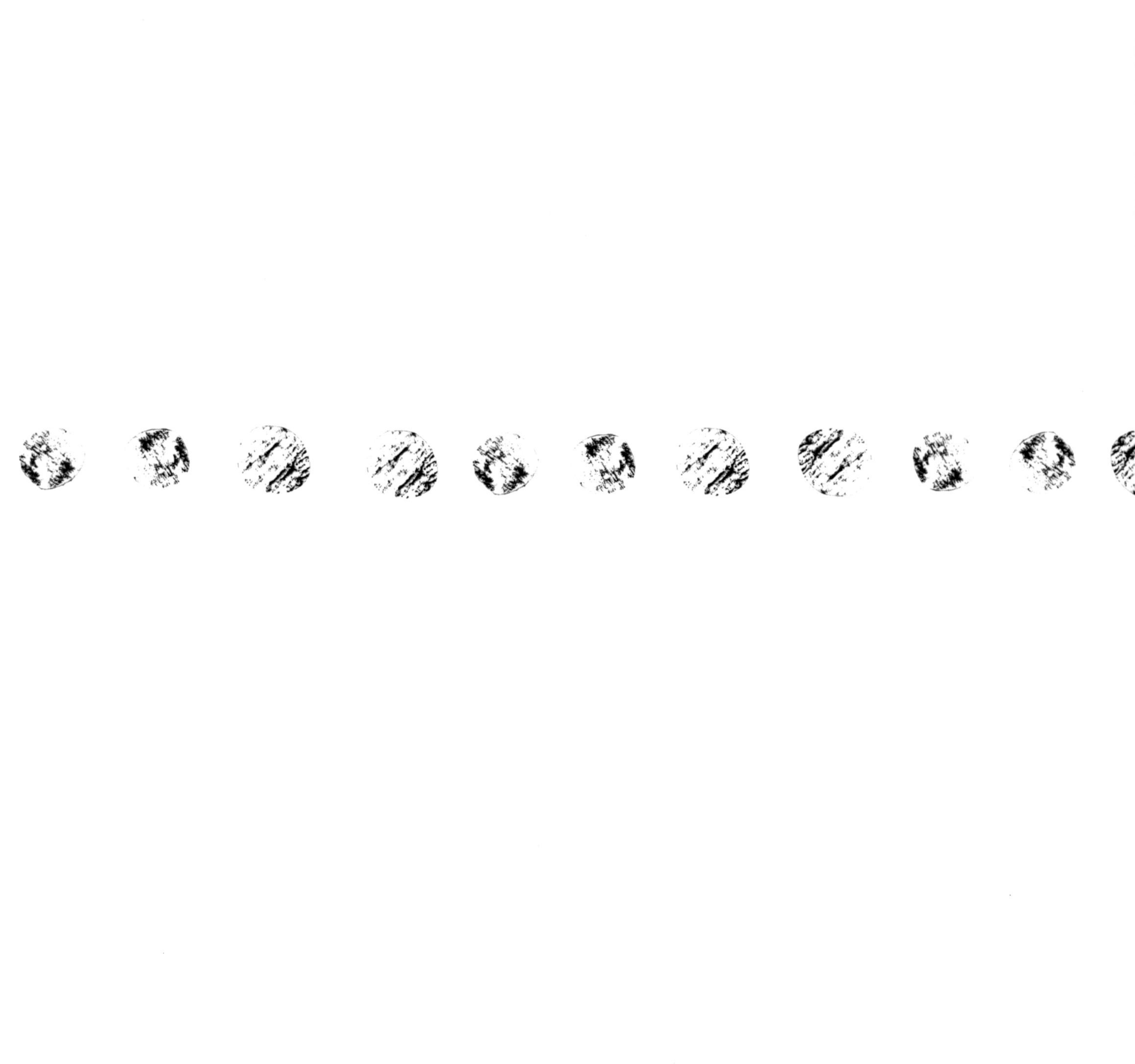

MY BED AND ME

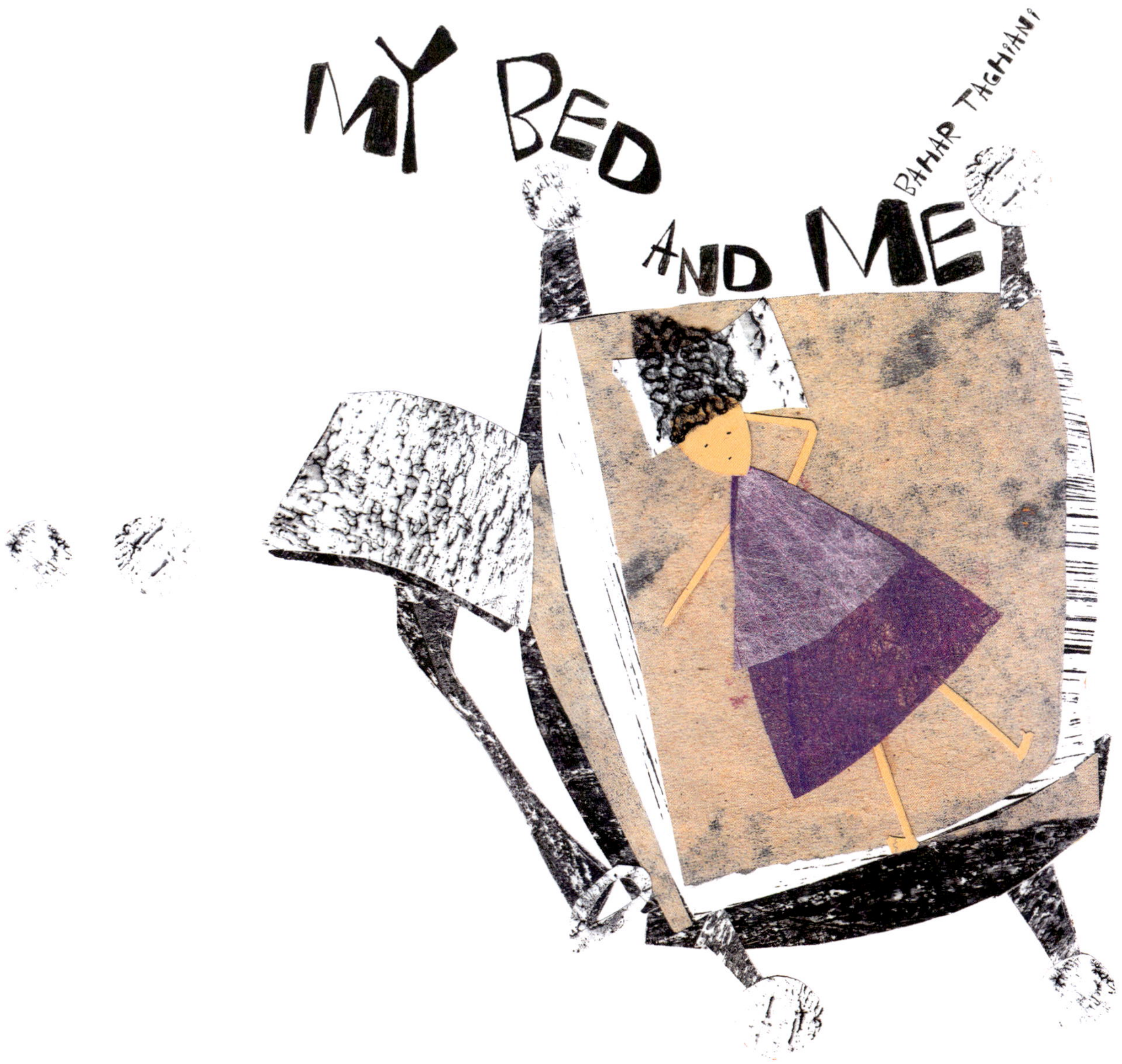

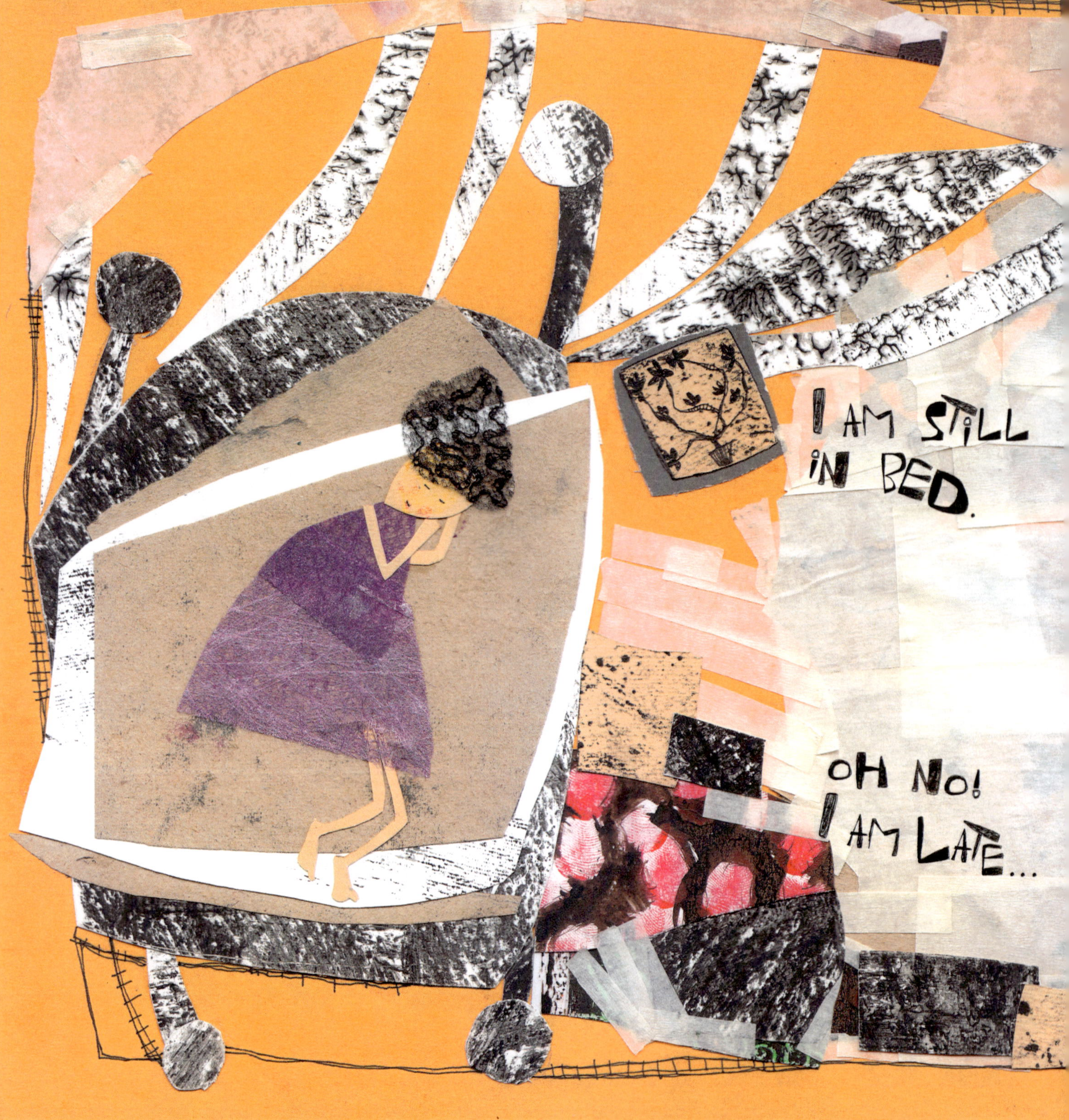

I AM STILL IN BED.
OH NO! I AM LATE...

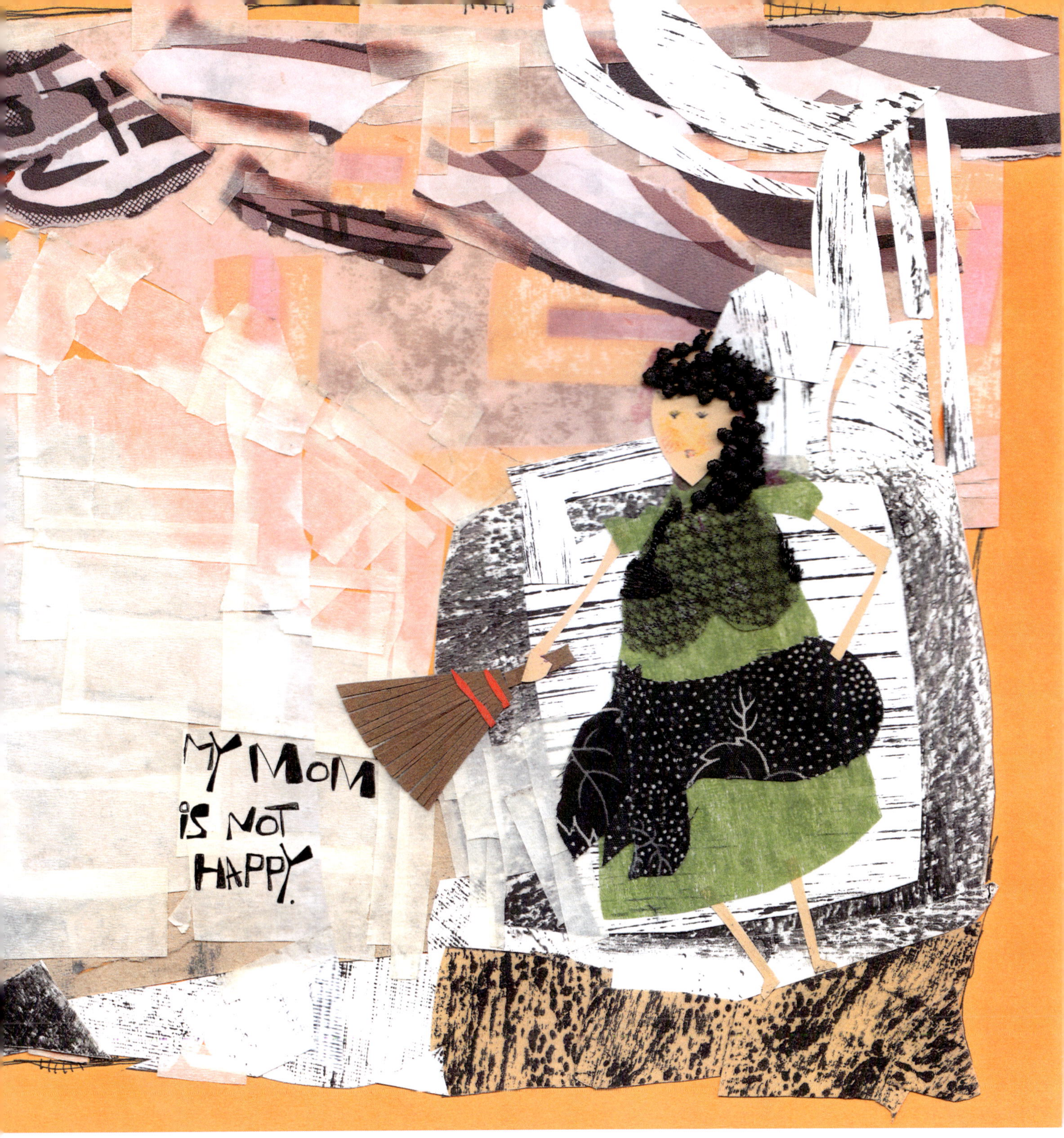
MY MOM
IS NOT
HAPPY.

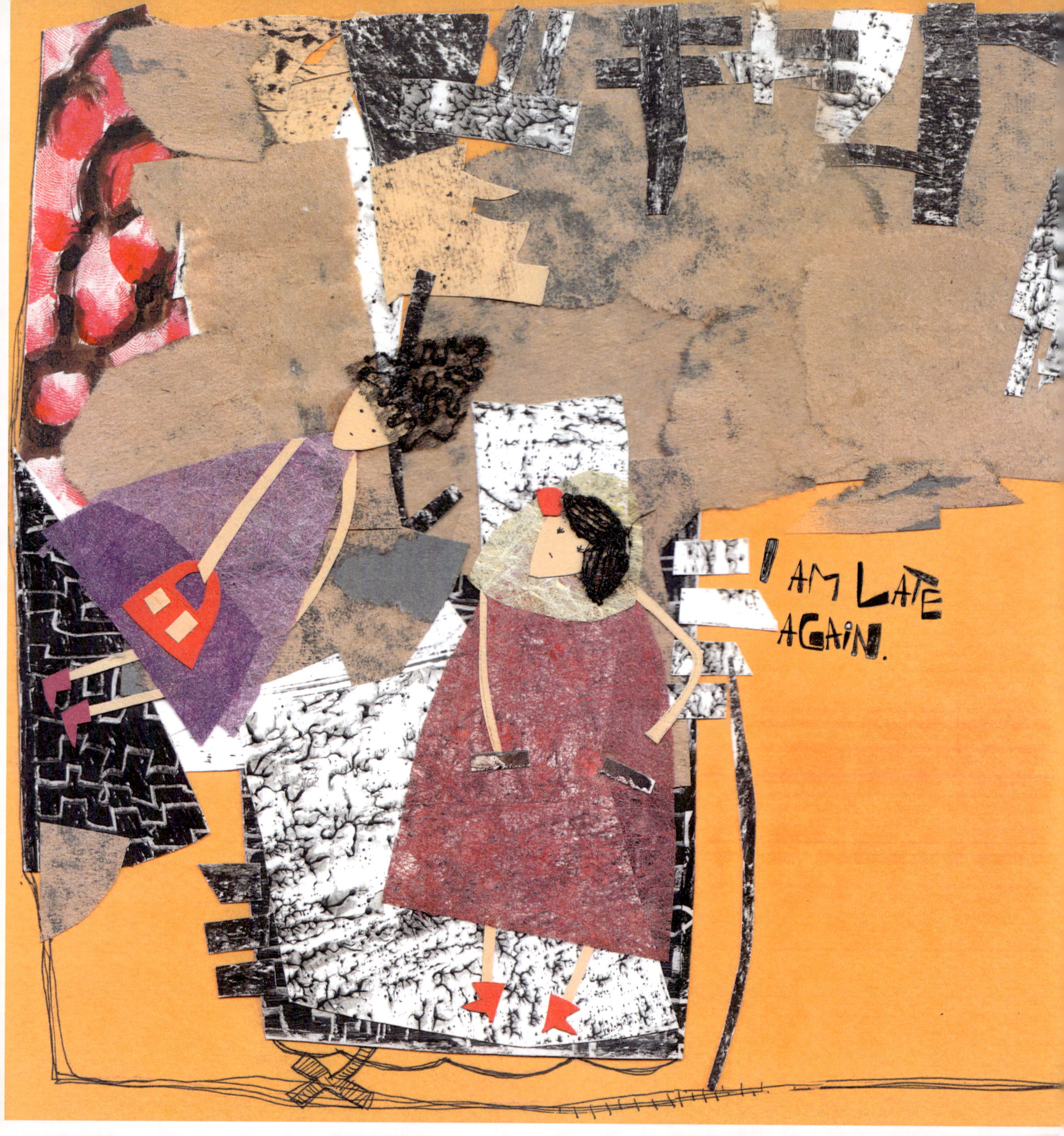

I AM LATE
AGAIN.

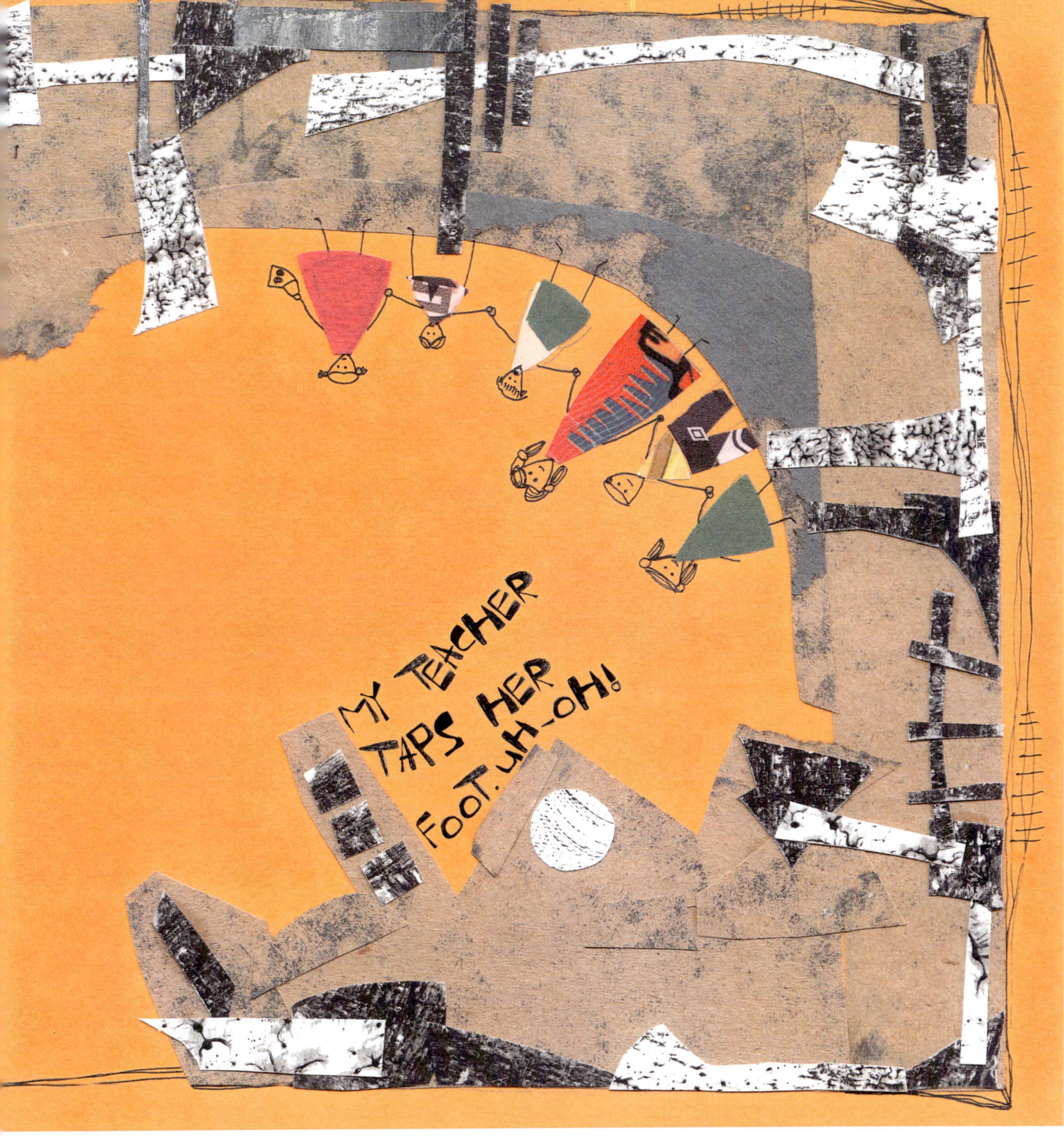

MY TEACHER TAPS HER FOOT. UH-OH!

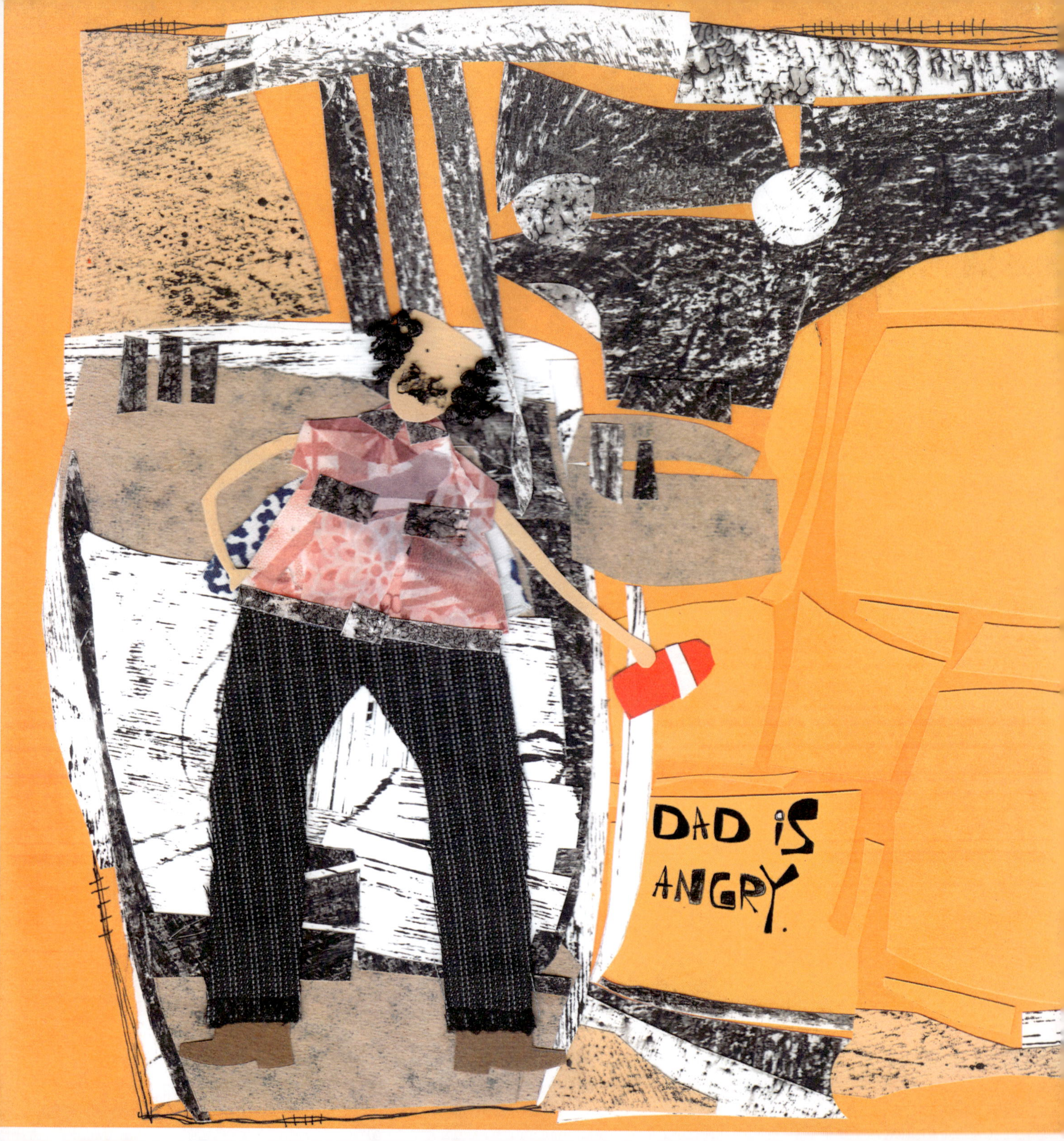

DAD IS ANGRY.

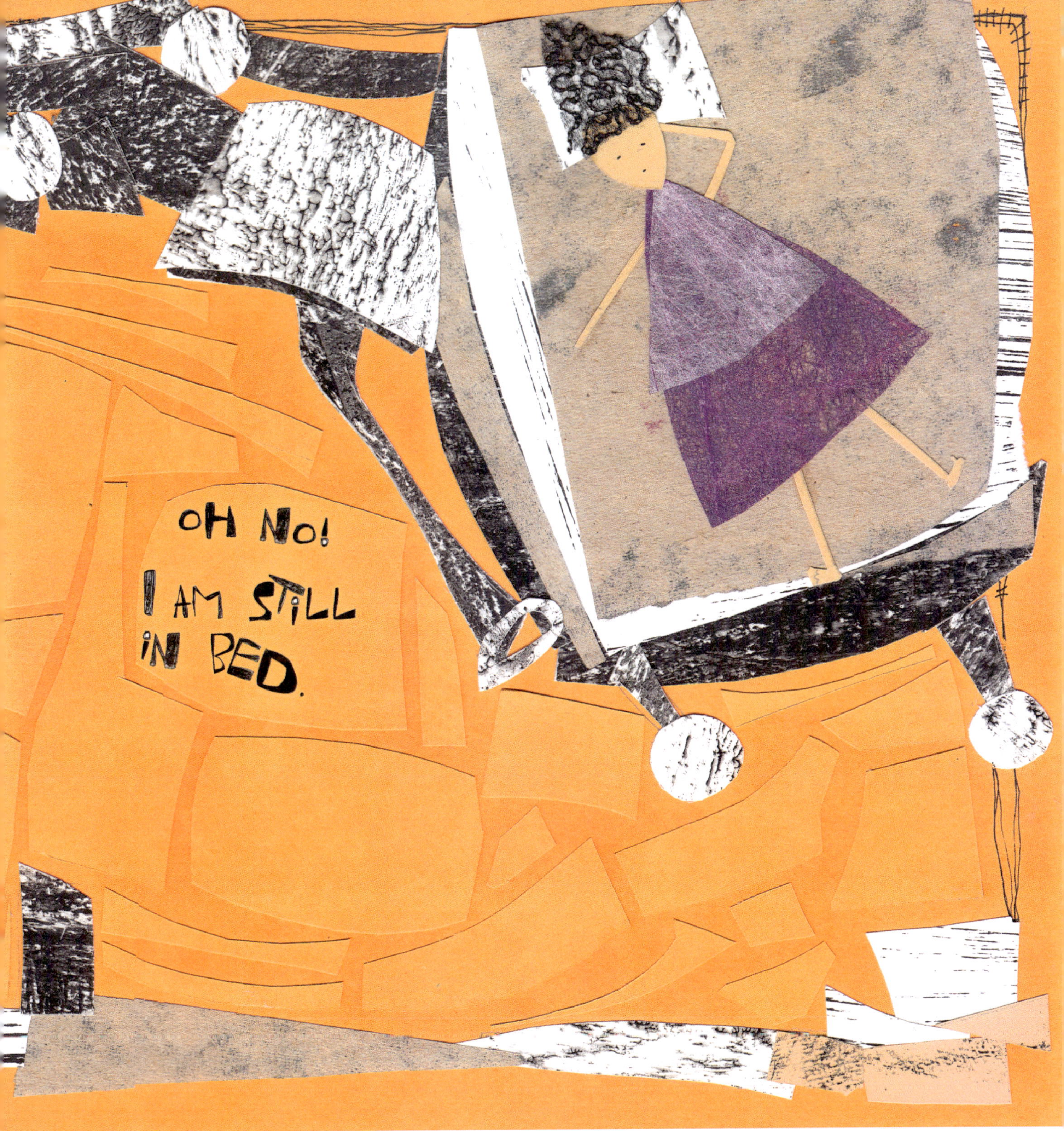
OH NO!
I AM STILL
IN BED.

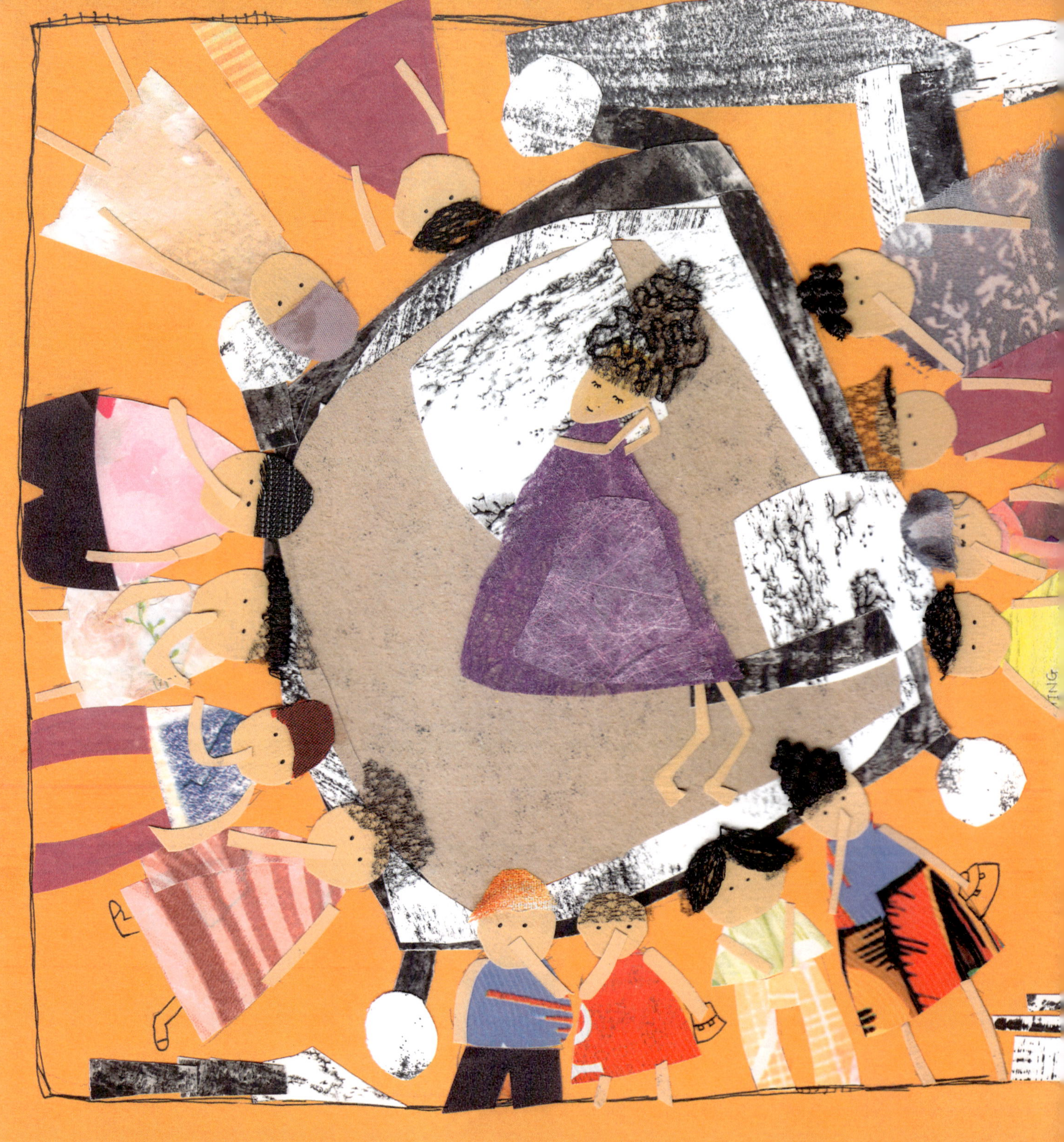

MY BED TAKES ME TO SCHOOL!

ALL MY CLASSMATES ARE STARING AT ME.

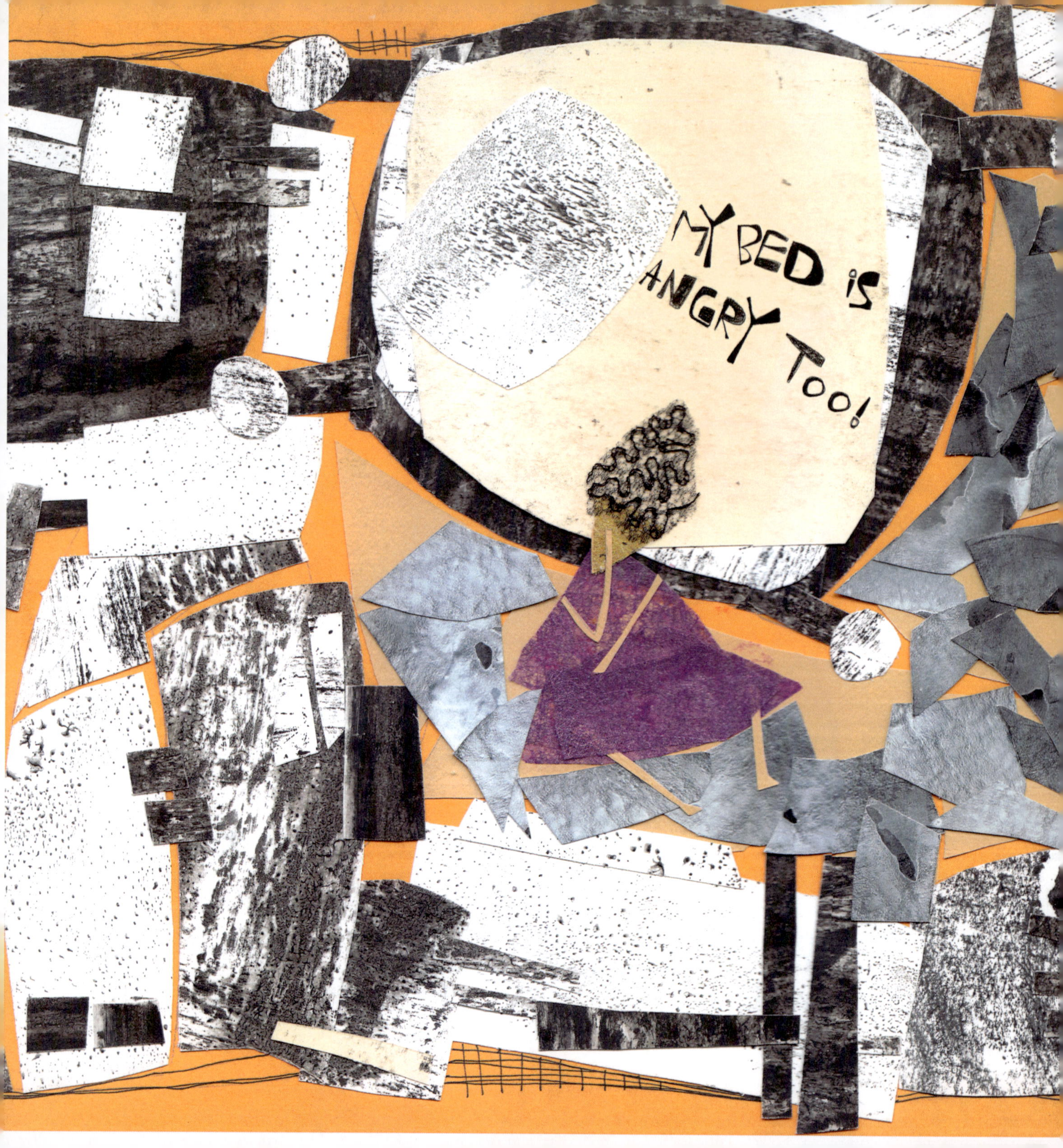
MY BED is
ANGRY Too!

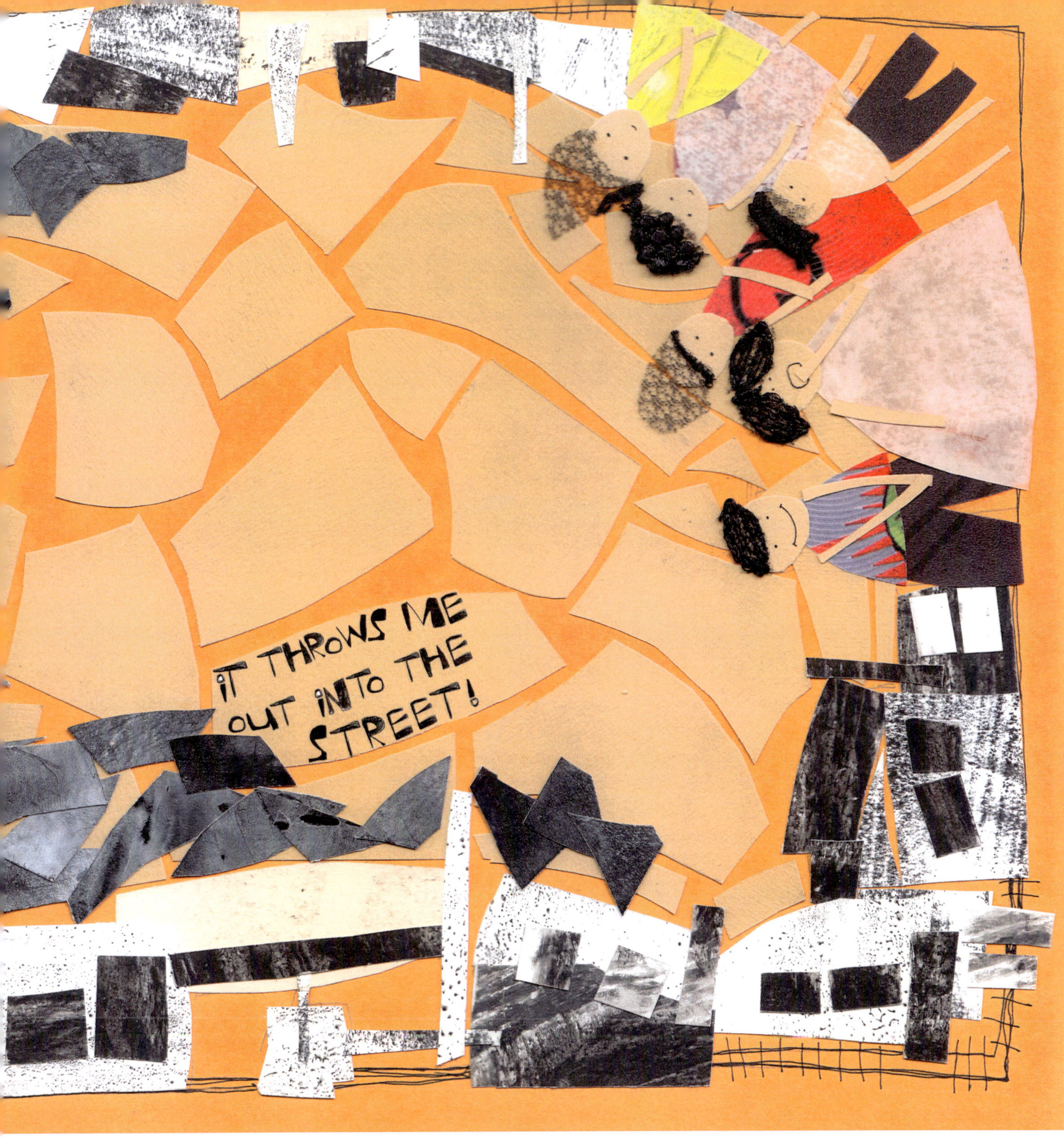

IT THROWS ME OUT INTO THE STREET!

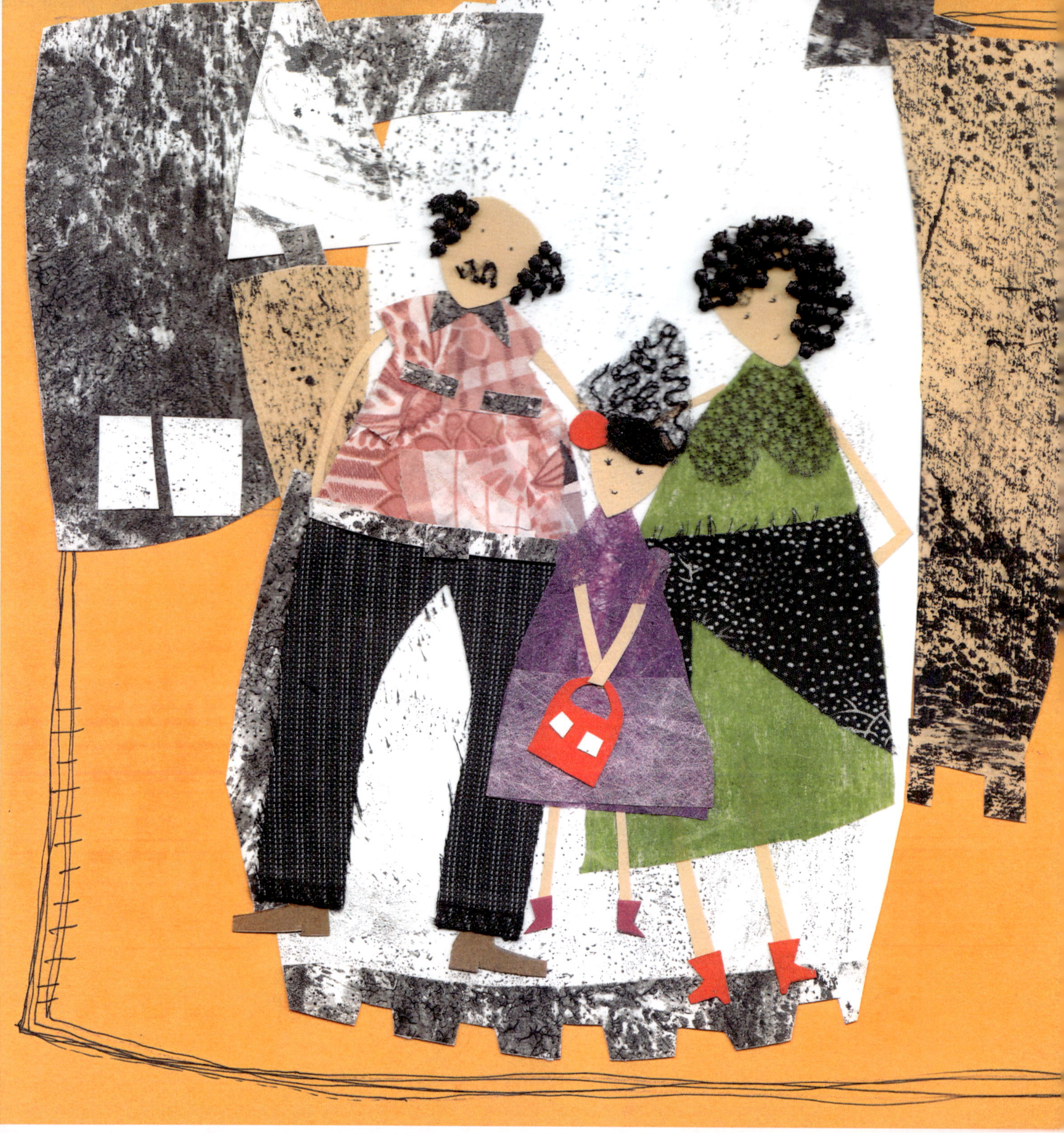

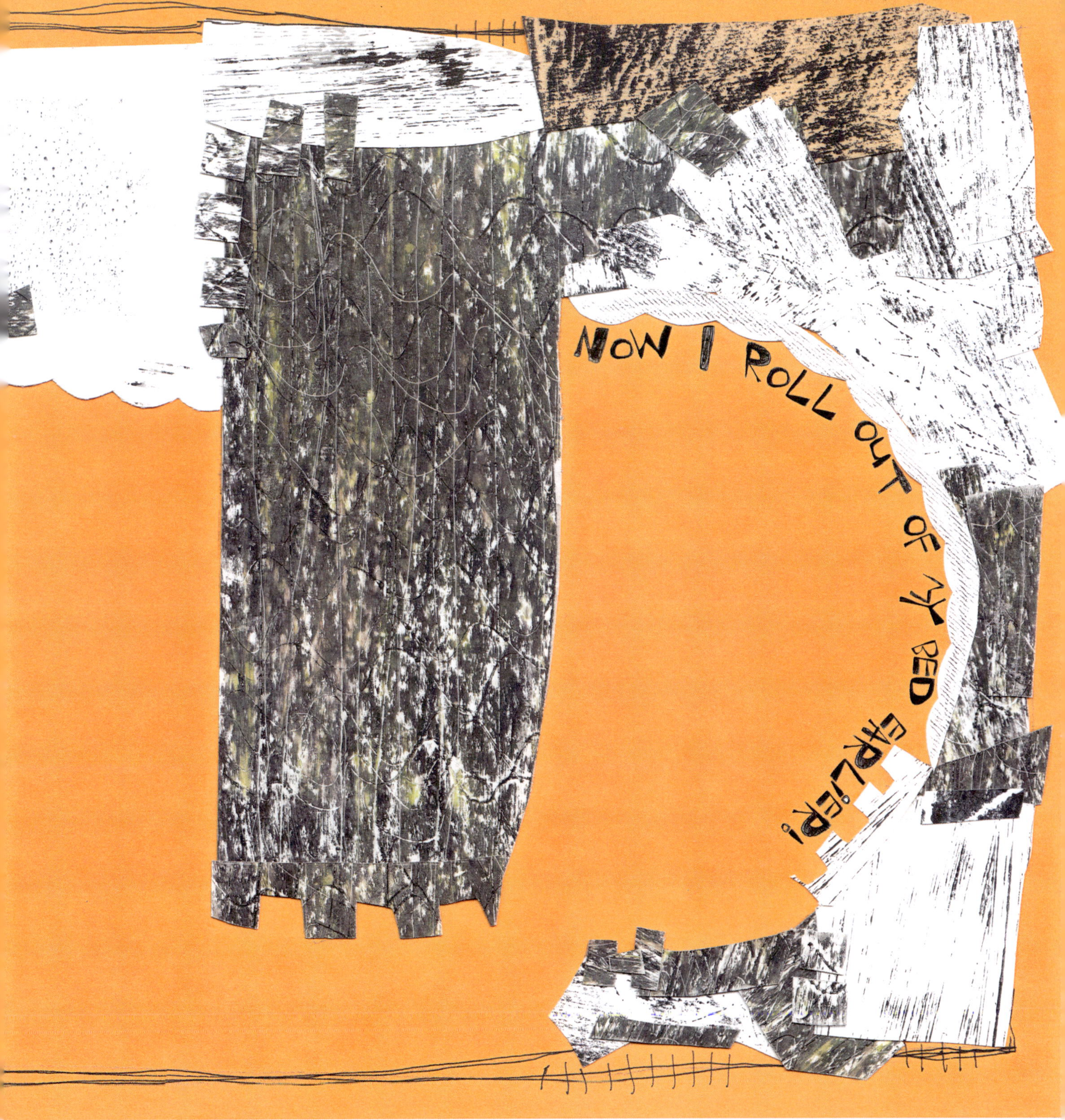

NOW I ROLL OUT OF MY BED EARLIER!

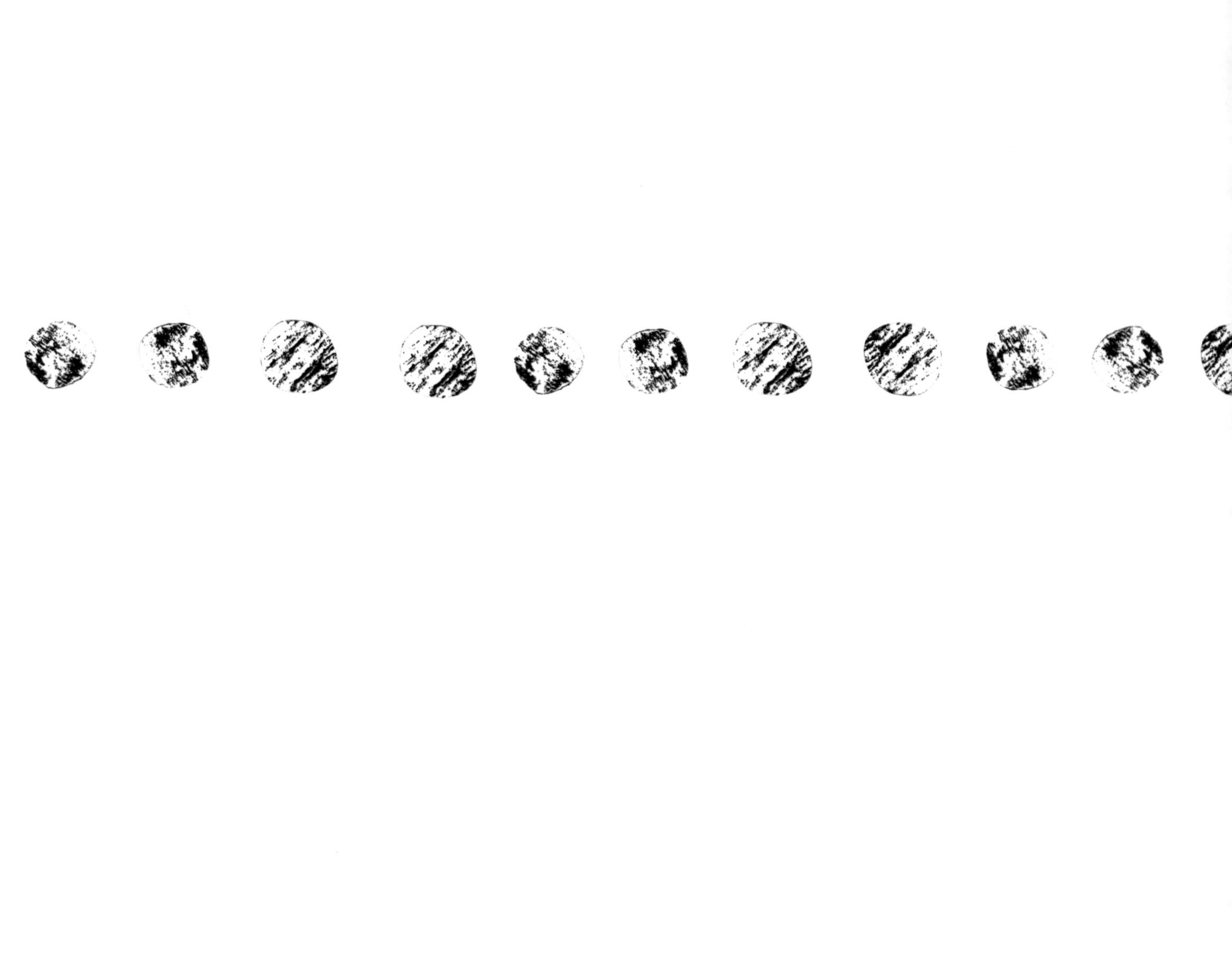

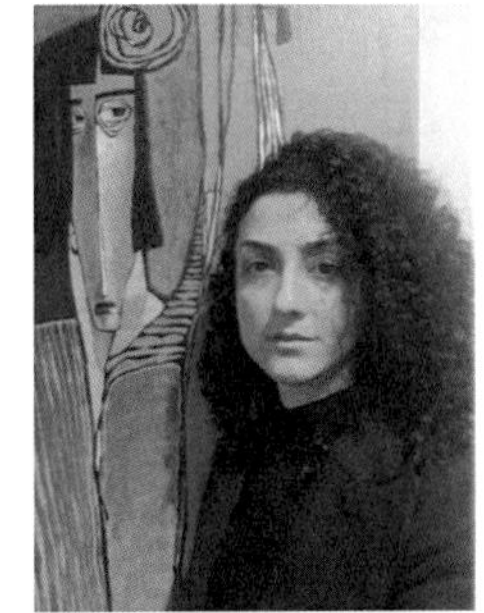

Bahar Taghiani is an illustrator and visual artist whose love for visual imagery began in early childhood. She started by creating characters out of pieces of paper, placing them in imagined stories, and bringing them to life. Today, her artworks are primarily created using mediums such as acrylic, collage, colored pencil, and watercolor, drawing inspiration from her perception of the world around her. Bahar is an award-winning artist, recognized by UNICEF for her illustration in the competition "Children on the Eve of New Year."

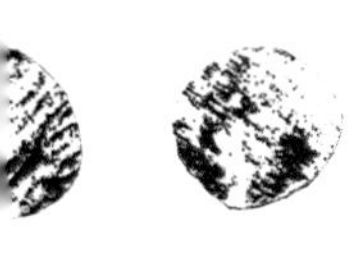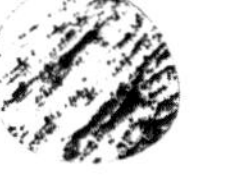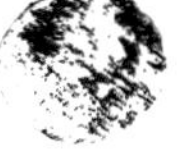

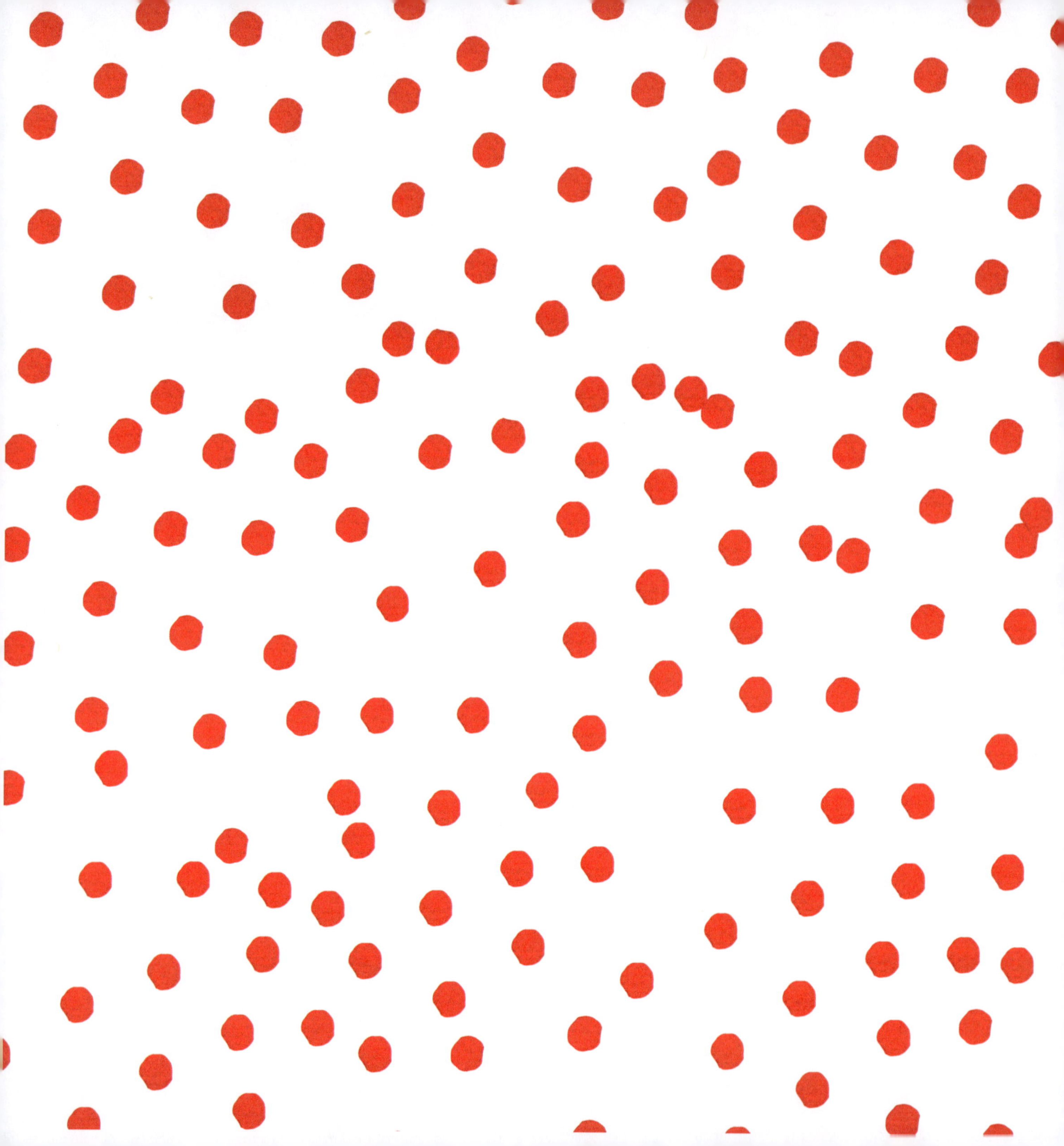

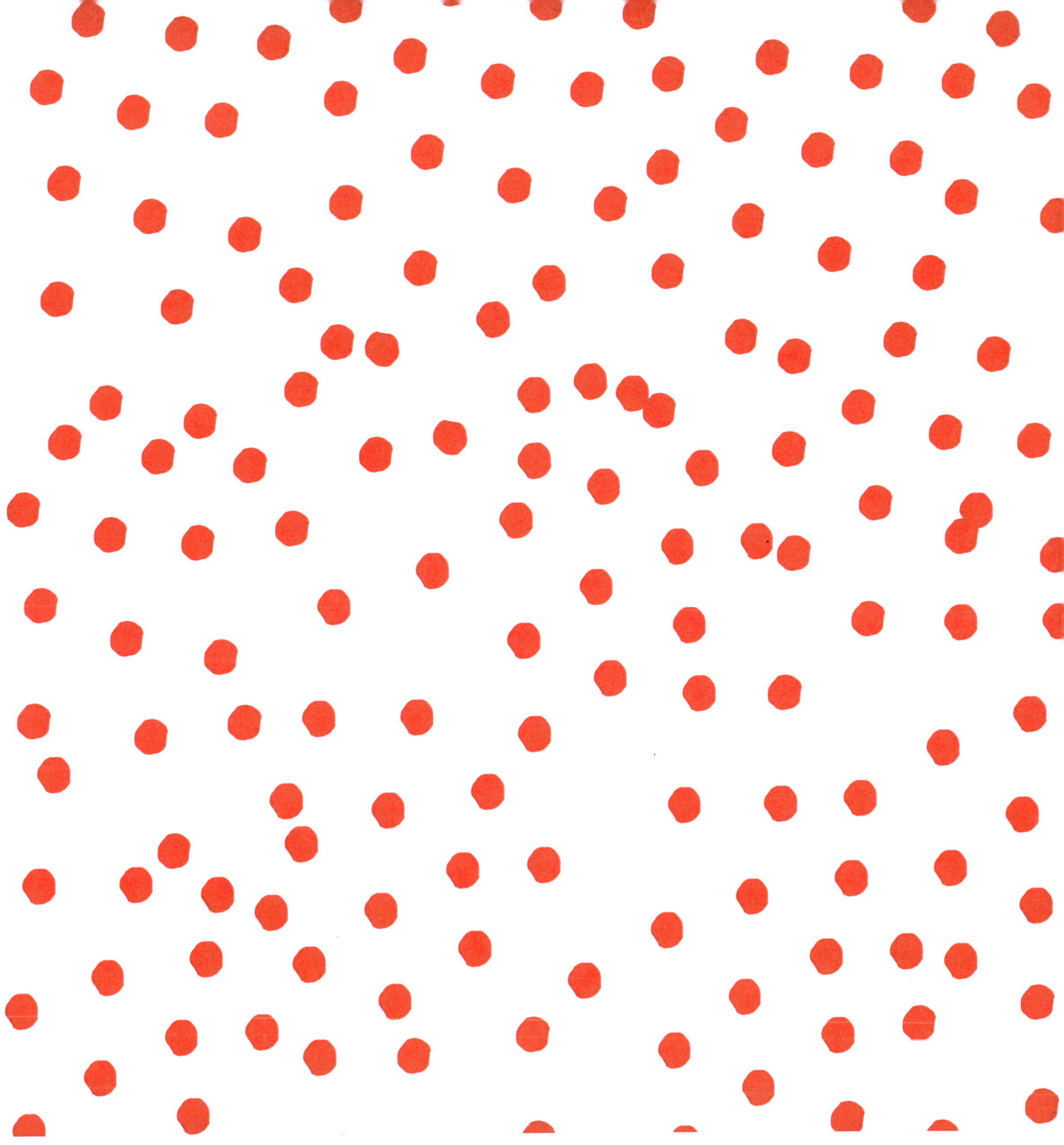

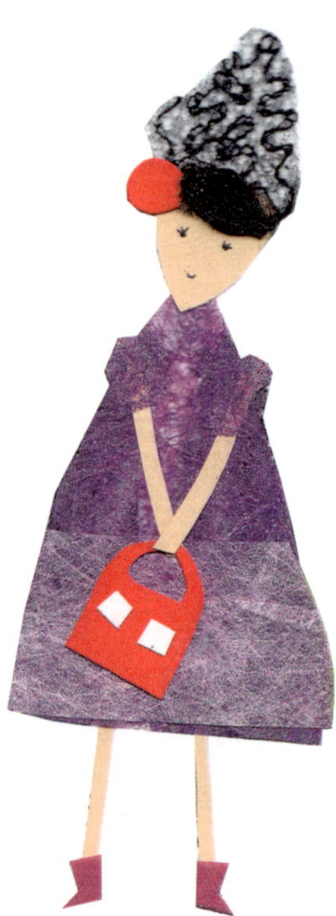